MARIE M. CLAY

RUNNING RECORDS

For Classroom Teachers

PEARSON

Heinemann

Contents

1 | About Running Records

This book begins by describing some of the key ideas about using Running Records as an assessment of text reading. In subsequent sections it introduces how to take and score a reliable record, and how that record can be interpreted.

Reading the messages

Running Records provide an assessment of *text reading*, and are designed to be taken as a child reads orally from any text. The successful early reader brings his speech to bear on the interpretation of print. His vocabulary, sentence patterns and pronunciation of words provide indispensable clues for recognising printed words.

The young reader learns to follow the directional conventions of written language and until he learns something about how to move across print he is unlikely to make much progress with trying to read.

Gradually the successful beginning reader becomes attentive to the visual detail of words, spaces, letters and the sounds that are represented. At the same time he begins to pull more than one kind of information into the 'simple' act of reading. This early phase in learning to read can be understood as laying down several layers of knowledge that are the foundation of subsequent success.

Another view

Typically children's progress in learning to read is measured by testing the number of letters, or sounds, or words they know. Yet most of the time in classrooms they are asked to read continuous texts: they are asked to put together the messages transmitted by the letters, sounds or words. If Running Records are taken in a systematic way they provide evidence of how well children are directing their knowledge of letters, sounds and words to understanding the messages in the text.

An example from a child's reading of text (page 4) explains the task. Look at the difficulty of the text. Count the child's errors and self-corrections (SC). Think about the things that challenged this child, the substitutions he made, and what made him correct the last substitution. The record provides evidence of the kinds of things that this child can do with the information he can get from print.

Records are taken to guide teaching

Running Records capture what the readers said and did while reading books or texts. Having taken the record teachers can review what happened immediately, leading to a teaching decision on the spot, or at a later time as they plan for next lessons. They can judge what the reader already knows, what the reader attended to, and what the reader overlooked. They can assess how well each reader is pulling together what he or she already knows about letters, sounds and words in order to get to the messages. This kind of information allows teachers to prompt, support and challenge individual learners. The records allow teachers to describe how children are working on a text.

Teachers may have to learn some new terms and concepts in order to interpret their Running Records. The procedures are simple, yet what they record can challenge them to think with greater clarity about the progress of beginning readers.

Records are taken to assess text difficulty

One use of a Running Record is as a check on whether students are working on material of appropriate difficulty, neither too difficult nor too easy, but offering a suitable level of challenge to the learner.

Records are taken to capture progress

From the time a child tries to retell a story from the pictures in a book until the reader has become a silent reader, Running Records, taken at selected intervals, can plot a path of progress. As teachers try to interpret each Running Record, they take into account the difficulty level of the text and make sound judgements about the reader's progress up through a gradient of difficulty in texts. A desirable path of progress shows that learners are meeting the challenges of increasingly difficult texts.

The examples in this book are selected to demonstrate how Running Records can be used on both simple and more advanced texts.

A child reading a text well

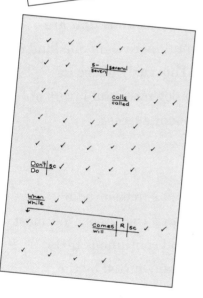

The Wolf and the Seven Little Kids

retold by **Fran Hunia**
pictures by **Nina Price**

Once there was a mother goat who had seven little kids. One day, she called to her kids. "I have to go out to look for food," she said. "Do not open the door while I'm away, or the wolf will come in and eat you up."

29

A Running Record of reading behaviour. Notice how the teacher's record is laid out in lines that match the text being read. The record provides a 'view' of how a text was read.

Compare two Running Records on the same text

This is a simple illustration of what a teacher could learn from Running Records. Peter and John read the same text and the records show that they need different emphases in their instruction.

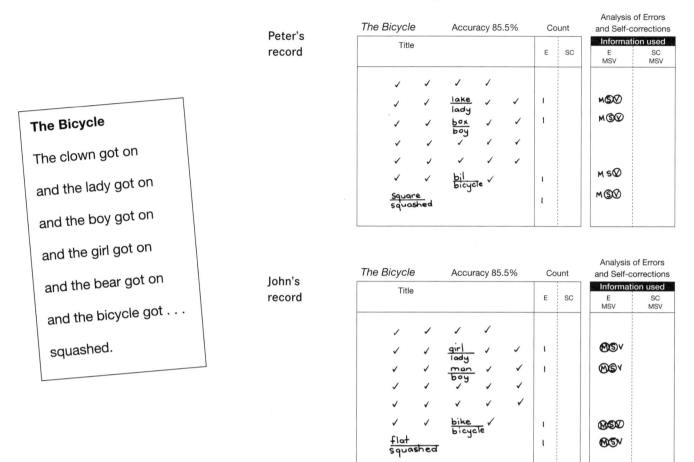

The Bicycle

The clown got on

and the lady got on

and the boy got on

and the girl got on

and the bear got on

and the bicycle got . . .

squashed.

Peter uses some visual information from the print and he is paying some attention to sentence structure (because his errors tend to belong to a class of words which could occur in the sentence up to the error). He does not react to the lack of meaning in what he says.

John is using language information and all his errors reflect the use of meaning and sentence structure. He does not seem to be aware of the mismatch between what he is saying and the visual information in the text.

This shows that Running Records can capture how beginning readers are putting together what they know in order to read text. We may question the quality of the text but it challenges the children to reveal how they are working on text.

2 Taking a Running Record

About three workshop training sessions with a teacher who is very familiar with Running Records are recommended for teachers before they begin to use this assessment technique. It takes more than self-teaching from a manual to achieve a high standard of observing, recording and interpreting. However, children do some unusual things, so further discussions with colleagues should be scheduled.

Congenial conditions

In every sense this activity of taking Running Records should be as relaxed as sharing a book with a child. Invite children to read to you and tell them that you will be writing down some things. That gives them a little warning that for the next few minutes you are not going to teach. Those teachers who have practised with a wide variety of children and are at ease in taking Running Records will be the teachers who get the most informative records and will make the fairest interpretations.

What does skilled record-taking look like?

A classroom teacher should, ideally, be able to sit down beside a child with a blank sheet of paper (or see pages 30-31) and take a Running Record when the moment is right. Teachers should practise until it is as easy as that. Any text, at any time, as and when appropriate, should be the aim. Then this technique will be flexible enough to suit any classroom conditions. It will also be probable that the teacher's recording can be relied upon to be a 'true account'. (See page 10 for another example.)

Teachers should prepare themselves to get the record down while the child is reading. At first, the easy-to-notice things are recorded; with practice it becomes easy to record any child reading any text, at any time. When they can record the essentials, teachers find it easy to also note what the child said about the task, or how they moved across print, and other interesting things like turning back several pages and correcting an earlier error. With practice teachers get more information from their observations and records.

At first, the task seems to require one's whole attention without interruption but before long teachers become bold enough to work in a busy classroom. If a teacher needs to say, at the foot of a page, 'Just a minute; I'm a bit slow today', children will wait. Before long the rest of the class comes to accept the taking of Running Records as common practice and will learn to leave the teacher alone to get the job done.

Two things to avoid

Teachers should learn to take Running Records in ways that will allow them to use this technique — with any child on any text, at any time.

Printed text: There is not enough room on a pre-printed page of text for the teacher to record all the unusual things that can occur. Many teachers are surprised to find that a printed text often will not allow all of the child's behaviours to be recorded. This is because a Running Record is not just about right or wrong words; it is about a lot more than that. Beginning readers do not keep closely to the text: they sometimes leave out large sections and insert things that are not there; they change direction, go back over what they have read, and confuse themselves.

A Running Record needs to capture all the behaviour that helps us to interpret what the child was probably doing. Everything the child said and did tells us something: when the reading is correct, what his hands and eyes were doing, the comments he made, when he re-ran a line of text, and so on. The aim is this: after a Running Record a teacher should be able to 'hear the reading again' when reviewing the record.

Limiting observations to a few select texts pre-printed on a scoring sheet will provide less usable information. Readers do very interesting things as they attempt to get an acceptable message from the pages of a book, and the object of Running Records is *to get valid records of how children are arriving at their decisions*. Authors and publishers try to 'make it easy' for teachers by providing pre-printed texts but children's problem-solving on texts is too diverse to conform to a published layout. A printed text encourages teachers to attend only to right and wrong responses, and to ignore how the child is arriving at these decisions.

Tape recording: Avoid the use of a tape-recorder. Having to tape the assessment is a crutch to be got rid of as soon as possible, so why not start without it. Tape-recording may seem easier at first, but it limits the analysis because a tape does not record visual information — how the child moved, seemed puzzled, peered at the print or looked at the ceiling.

Select children who will make practising easier

Practise on a range of *average* readers who are about one year into school, as many as you can. Avoid practising on higher or lower progress readers until you become skilled. Good readers go too fast, and struggling readers produce complex records. For each child make records of two or three little books, or text pieces with about 100–200 words in each, and have the child read each whole story or text. At the early reading level when the child is reading the simplest books, the numbers of words may fall below 100 but if three texts are read this will be satisfactory even though the extracts themselves are short. Once a teacher knows how to take Running Records it should take about 10 minutes to get three samples. Sharing early records with a teacher who uses them a lot will produce useful discussions.

Select some texts for practising

1   Any texts can be used for Running Records — books, stories, information texts, children's published writing — but a good place to start is with a familiar text that the child has read once or twice before. This text will provide evidence of how the reader is bringing different processes and skills together. A classroom teacher would probably select something the child has recently read in class. *The prime purpose of a Running Record is to understand more about how children are using what they know to get to the messages of the text, or in other words what reading processes they are using.*

   Children who are proficient readers can be assessed for a different purpose — to see how they read a new, unseen text revealing a level of achievement.

2   It is a good idea to start each assessment with a text that is easy for this child. An 'easy level' book will also be easy for teachers to record as they rehearse their recording techniques.

3   The teacher may want to know how the child performs on a challenging text. Sometimes the teacher discovers that the child can work at a higher level than that teacher anticipated. A challenging text could show whether the reader recognises the need for problem-solving and what kinds of problem-solving this reader tries. However if the challenges are too great the record will not show how the reading process comes together, but how and when it falls apart.

A text at each of the easy, instructional or hard levels will provide the necessary evidence for a concise summary of where that child is in his learning. The terms *easy*, *instructional* and *hard* used in Running Records do not describe the characteristics of the text itself. They *describe how a particular child read the text*. They do not say anything about how another child will read that text. Whether it is easy or instructional or difficult is determined entirely by how well the child was able to work on it. When publishers suggest some order of difficulty in their books they are usually estimating how children in general might find these books. Look for evidence of whether the publishers trialled their books on a sample of children and whether those children were anything like the children you teach.

When a child reads a text at between 90 and 94 percent accuracy level, this is called an instructional level. The record will contain evidence of problem-solving because it will contain some error. Teachers can then observe how children work at monitoring their own reading. In the young reader we can hear and record most of the problem-solving (also called processing the information) but as readers become more proficient more of the processing is hidden from view, worked out in the child's head before a response is made.

For important educational decisions it is not enough for teachers to assess children only on their current reading books. Recording their performance at three levels of text difficulty:
- an easy text (95 to 100 percent correct)
- an instructional text (90 to 94 percent correct)
- and a hard text (80 to 89 percent correct)

is a more reliable way to establish the level of text to be used for instruction. This more careful approach would be used for important educational decisions like moving children to different groups, observing children with particular difficulties, selecting children for special and supplementary assistance, making decisions about promotion, or for a school survey of achievement. Three levels of difficulty must be obtained for research studies.

Older proficient readers become fast readers, too fast for the teacher to make ticks (checks) for every word. Then the observer can give up recording the correct responding, and, keeping strictly to the layout and lines of the text, record all the processing the reader does to monitor, solve words and self-correct. This is a compromise made only for very fast readers. The record needs to be analysed immediately for it is hard to recapture the 'reading' from such a limited record.

3 How to Record What You See

Another book read well

The next record provides an illustration of many but not all of the recording techniques. The record must mimic the layout of the lines in the text the child is reading.

Text	Record
"A bee!" said Baby Bear.	✓ ✓ ✓ ✓ ✓
"Where is he going?"	✓ ✓ ✓ ✓
The bee went into a tree.	✓ ✓ ✓ ✓ ✓ bush | R | SC
	tree | |
Baby Bear looked in the tree.	✓ ✓ looks | SC ✓ a | R | SC ✓
	looked| the | |
"Honey!" said Baby Bear.	✓ ✓ ✓ ✓
"Honey for me! Thank you,	✓ ✓ ✓ ✓ ✓
bee."	✓

Standard ways of recording are recommended to take care of almost all the unusual behaviours teachers might encounter. The conventions described have been widely used with children who are reading English. The recording is both easy for teachers and reliable as an assessment, and is not limited to a particular theory of literacy learning. However, in any interpretation of the record, the teacher's theory of literacy learning begins to become involved. (This is discussed on page 21.)

Why use standard procedures?

If a teacher claims that a child read a text above the 94 percent level of accuracy, we need to be assured that this had been obtained according to common practice. If this is not true then calculations and comparisons do not have any meaning. This is a very important statement. Teachers want to be able to compare Running Records one with another. Either they want to know how Johnny's record today compares with his earlier records, or they need to make some teaching decision about several children and want to compare one reader with another. To make comparisons teachers need to have a common standard for taking records, for describing what they observe, for calculating the scores and interpreting the record.

The aim is to take a full record, recording and scoring it reliably so comparisons can be made.

However, teachers should also try to write down the comments children make as they read the book, working out loud, talking to themselves, being surprised, giving some rationale for what they did, and any personal reactions — these support the interpretation of the record.

Conventions for recording

1 Mark every word read correctly with a tick (or check).

A record of the first five pages of the 'Ready to Read' (1963) book *Early in the Morning* that was 100 percent correct would look like this. (The lines indicate page breaks.)

Bill is asleep.	✓	✓	✓
'Wake up, Bill,'	✓	✓	✓
said Peter.	✓	✓	
Sally is asleep.	✓	✓	✓
'Wake up, Sally,'	✓	✓	✓
said Mother.	✓	✓	
Father is shaving.	✓	✓	✓

2 Record a wrong response with the text under it.

Child:	*home*	
Text:	house	[One error]

3 If a child tries several times to read a word, record all his trials.

Child:	*here*	*h—*	*home*	
Text:	house			[One error]

Child:	*h—*	*ho—*	✓	
Text:	home			[No error]

4 If a child succeeds in correcting a previous error this is recorded as 'self-correction' (written SC).

Note that the examples in **3** did not result in self-corrections.

Child:	*where*	*when*	SC	
Text:	were			[No error]

5 If no response is given to a word it is recorded with a dash. Insertion of a word is recorded over a dash.

No response   Insertion

Child:	—	Child:	here
Text:	house	Text:	—	[In each case one error]

6 If the child baulks, unable to proceed because he is aware he has made an error and cannot correct it, or because he cannot attempt the next word, he is told the word (written T).

Child:	home	
Text:	house	T	[One error]

7 An appeal for help (A) from the child is turned back to the child for further effort before using T as in **6** above. Say 'You try it.'

Child:	—	A	here
Text:	house		T	[One error]

8 Sometimes the child gets into a state of confusion and it is necessary to extricate him. The most detached method of doing this is to say 'Try that again', marking TTA on the record. This would not involve any teaching, but the teacher may indicate where the child should begin again.

It is a good idea to put square brackets around the first set of muddled behaviour, enter the TTA, remember to count that as one error only (see page 17), and then begin a fresh record of the problem text. An example of this recording would be:

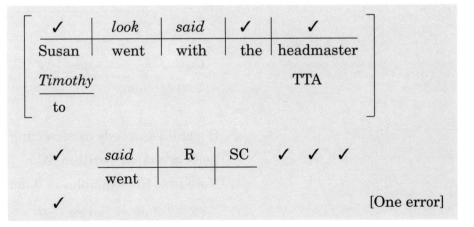

12

9 Repetition (R) is not counted as error behaviour. Sometimes it is used to confirm a previous attempt. Often it results in self-correction. It is useful to record it as it often indicates how much sorting out the child is doing. 'R', standing for repetition, is used to indicate repetition of a word, with R_2 or R_3 indicating the number of repetitions. If the child goes back over a group of words, or returns to the beginning of the line or sentence in his repetition, the point to which he returns is shown by an arrow.

Child:	Here is the home	R	SC	
Text:	Here is the house			[No error]

10 Sometimes the child rereads the text (repetition) and corrects some but not all errors. The following example shows the recording of this behaviour.

Child:	a	SC	house	R	
Text:	the		home		One error / One SC

11 Directional attack on the printed text is recorded by telling the child to 'Read it with your finger'.

Left to right	L $\longrightarrow$ R	Snaking	
Right to left	L $\longleftarrow$ R	Bottom to top	↑

12 Other behaviours. The conventions for recording and scoring relate only to correct responses, errors, and self-corrections. Other behaviours include pausing, sounding out the letters, and splitting words into parts. Research evidence has shown that teachers' records of such behaviours are much less reliable and cannot be included in the Count or Analysis scoring.

A Running Record from a child who is making many errors is hard to record and score but the rule is to record all the behaviour, and analyse objectively what is recorded.

Check directional movement

Sometimes you may notice signs that tell you the young reader is not following the directional rules for attending to print. To check on this select a few lines of print during the reading and say to the child, 'Read this part with your finger.' A brief observation will often be sufficient but extend the observation if you need to understand more about this behaviour. Even if teachers do not find pointing a desirable teaching prompt, they will still need to collect some evidence of starting points, direction of scanning, and lapses or confusions from beginning readers.

Describe the reading behaviour recorded

Immediately following the reading and before you begin to analyse the detail of the record, write a few lines on what you just observed, your intuitive summation of the child's reading, at the end of the record. This should be an overall reaction. Comment on what the reader did well. Was the reading done at a good pace, or was it slow, or too fast? Are things in balance or out of balance in your judgement? How well is this child reading? Attend particularly to progress over previous readings.

Assessment and comprehension

Running Records should be valued because they adhere to good assessment practices. Some teachers wish to add retelling or comprehension questions to the taking of a Running Record. Here are some comments and cautions.

- Comprehension is very dependent upon the difficulty level of the text. It makes no sense to assess comprehension on a hard text, nor on an easy text. If the text level is instructional then that tells the teacher to teach for understanding.
- Because different teachers ask different questions the assessment is weakened.
- The answers to comprehension questions depend more upon the difficulty of the question asked than on the child's reading, according to research.

The reliability and validity of these assessments are not improved when teachers cannot agree on the scoring or when what teachers do is non-standard, like asking questions which differ in content or form.

Conversation with a child about the story after taking Running Records adds to the teacher's understanding of the reader in useful ways.

A record before scoring

The page from Paul's reading (below) could have been made on a blank piece of paper. It shows part of the Running Record that was taken, only 55 running words. The scoring of errors (E) and self-corrections (SC) on the right-hand side is discussed on pages 16 and 17. Reread the text as the child read it.

Paul's record

Page of text	Running Record	E	SC
The milk ran	✓ ✓ ✓		
all over the ground.	✓ ✓ ✓ g– / ground | garden		
And there was the woman	✓ threw / there | th– | th– / T | ✓ ✓ R ✓ R₂		
with the magpie's tail in her hand.	✓ ✓ ✓ ✓ ✓ ✓		
"Woman, give me back my tail!"	W– / Woman | R₄ | ✓ | g– / give | get | go ✓ ✓ ✓ ✓		
cried the magpie.	✓ ✓ ✓		
"I'll pin it on and fly back	✓ put / pin | pull | ✓ ✓ R the | R / and | SC | ✓ ✓		
to my mother and father.	✓ ✓ ✓ ✓ ✓		
If you don't give me back my tail	✓ ✓ ✓ ✓ ✓ ✓ ✓		
I'll eat the cabbages in your garden.	✓ ✓ ✓ c– / cabbages | cabbage | R ✓ ✓ ✓		

Count

The teacher made this summary in her own words:

Generally used meaning at challenging words and often used structure.
When approximating he usually checked further, often by rereading, and this led to a number of self-corrections. His approximations show that he is mainly using initial letters and he needs to search further. He reads with phrasing and retold the story confidently.

NB Check out his spelling approximations in writing!

4 How to Score Errors and Self-corrections

Review the running records of the child's behaviour on his current book and consider what was happening as the child read.

Some conventions for scoring the records

In counting the numbers of errors, some arbitrary decisions must be made but the following have been found workable.

1   Credit the child with any correct or corrected words.

Child:	to	the	shops	
Text:	for	the	bread	
Score:	✗	✓	✗	[Two errors]

2   There is no penalty for trials which are eventually correct.

A

Child:	want	won't	SC	
Text:	went			
Score:	—	—	✓	$\begin{bmatrix} \text{No error} \\ \text{One SC} \end{bmatrix}$

B

Child:	where	we	when	SC	
Text:	were				
Score:	—	—	—	✓	$\begin{bmatrix} \text{No error} \\ \text{One SC} \end{bmatrix}$

C

Child:	f–	fet	✓	
Text:	fright			
Score:	—	—	✓	[No error]

3   Insertions add errors so that a child can have more errors than there are words in a line.

Child:	The	train	went	toot,	toot,	toot	
Text:	The	little	engine	sighed			
Score:	✓	✗	✗	✗	✗	✗	[Five errors]

4   However, the child cannot receive a minus score for a page. The lowest page score is 0.

5   *Omissions.* If a line or sentence is omitted each word is counted as an error. If pages are omitted (perhaps because two pages were turned together) they are not counted as errors. Note that in this case, the number of words on the omitted pages must be deducted from the Running Words Total before calculation.

6 *Repeated errors.* If the child makes an error (e.g., 'run' for 'ran') and then substitutes this word repeatedly, it counts as an error every time; but substitution of a proper name (e.g., 'Mary' for 'Molly') is counted only the first time.

7 *Multiple errors and self-correction.* If a child makes two or more errors (e.g., reads a phrase wrongly) each word is an error. If he then corrects all these errors each corrected word is a self-correction.

8 *Broken words.* Where a word is pronounced as two words (e.g., a/way) even when this is backed up pointing as if it were two words, this is regarded as an error of pronunciation, not as a reading error unless what is said is matched to a different word. Such things as 'pitcher' for 'picture' and 'gonna' for 'going to' are counted as correct.

9 *Inventions* defeat the system. When the young child is creatively producing his own version of the story the scoring system finally breaks down and the judgement 'inventing' is recorded for that page, story or book.

10 *'Try that again.'* When the child is in a tangle this instruction, which does not involve teaching, can be given. It counts as one error and only the second attempt is scored (see page 12).

11 *Fewest errors.* If there are alternative ways of scoring responses a general principle is to choose the method that gives the fewest possible errors as in **B** below.

A	Child:	We	went	for	the	bread			
	Text:	You	went	to	the	shop	for	the	bread
	Score:	✗	✓	✗	✓	✗	✗	✗	✗ [Six errors]

B	Child:	We	went				for	the	bread
	Text:	You	went	to	the	shop	for	the	bread
	Score:	✗	✓	✗	✗	✗	✓	✓	✓ [Four errors]

Some other good practices

1 Do not try to analyse omissions and insertions.

2 Consider only the sentence up to and including the error.

3 Avoid analyses for which you have no theoretical support.

5 Quantifying the Running Record

Box 1

```
COUNT THE
RUNNING
WORDS


   150
```

Box 2

```
RATIO OF ERRORS
      TO
RUNNING WORDS
    Errors
  Running Words

     15
    150
    1 : 10
  One in ten
```

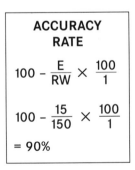

Box 3

ACCURACY
RATE

$$100 - \frac{E}{RW} \times \frac{100}{1}$$

$$100 - \frac{15}{150} \times \frac{100}{1}$$

$$= 90\%$$

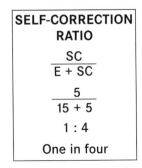

Box 4

SELF-CORRECTION
RATIO

$$\frac{SC}{E + SC}$$

$$\frac{5}{15 + 5}$$

$$1 : 4$$

One in four

Box 1: Count the words in the text, omitting titles.

Box 2: Count the errors, and enter the Error Ratio.

Box 3: Use the conversion table to find the Accuracy Rate.

Box 4: Work out the Self-correction Ratio.

Here is one way to think about self-corrections. There were 15 errors in 150 running words of text and the 5 self-corrections represent an extra 5 potential errors. Altogether there were 20 chances to make self-corrections so there were 5 self-corrections in 20 chances to self-correct.

The four boxes provide the calculations corresponding to the steps outlined above. The conversion table provides quick access to accuracy rates.

Conversion Table

Error Ratio	Percent Accuracy	
1:200	99.5	
1:100	99	
1:50	98	
1:35	97	
1:25	96	Good opportunities for teachers to observe children's processing of texts.
1:20	95	
1:17	94	
1:14	93	
1:12.5	92	
1:11.75	91	
1:10	90	
1:9	89	
1:8	87.5	
1:7	85.5	The reader tends to lose the support of the meaning of the text.
1:6	83	
1:5	80	
1:4	75	
1:3	66	
1:2	50	

Turn back to page 15 and score that Running Record. Put one count in the error column for every error and one count in the self-correction column for every self-correction. Total each column and work out the Error Ratio, the Accuracy Rate, and the Self-correction Ratio.

6 Records for Two Competent Readers

The next two examples capture the reading behaviours of two competent readers, and provide the reader with opportunities to 'read' back from the record what Emma and Claire did. The records are used to introduce an analysis of how the text was read.

Emma's reading

Emma read well and there were no self-corrections to analyse on this page of her Running Record. Yet her two errors allowed her teacher to identify two things to talk about. They could talk about the omission of 'as', how what she said sounded right but differed from what the author wrote. Important? Perhaps not. The second discussion would be about how she could work more effectively on the information in the middle of unfamiliar words, which may well be a crucial change in processing which she needs to make.

Emma's record

Analysis of Errors and Self-corrections

Page of Text	Running Record	Information used	
		E M S V	SC M S V
... resting their elbows on it, and talking over its	✓ ✓ ✓ ✓ ✓ ✓ ✓		
head. "Very uncomfortable for the Dormouse,"	✓. ✓ ✓ ✓ ✓		
thought Alice; "only as it's asleep, I suppose it	✓ ✓ ✓ —/as ✓ ✓ ✓ ✓		
doesn't mind."	✓ ✓.		
The table was a large one, but the three were all	✓ ✓ ✓ ✓ ✓ ✓ ✓ ✓ ✓		
crowded together at one corner of it. "No room!	✓ ✓ ✓ ✓ ✓ ✓. ✓ ✓		
No room!" they cried out when they saw Alice	✓ ✓ ✓ ✓ ✓ ✓ ✓ ✓		
coming. "There's plenty of room!" said Alice	✓. ✓ ✓ ✓ ✓ ✓		
indignantly, and she sat down in a large arm-chair	indently/indignantly ✓ ✓ ✓ ✓ ✓ ✓ ✓	M (S) (V)	
at one end of the table.	✓ ✓ ✓ ✓ ✓.		

Claire's reading

Claire made a number of errors on this text but she often self-corrected without any assistance. (Only a part of the record is shown and I simplified the record.)

Claire's record

Analysis of Errors and Self-corrections

Page of Text	Running Record	Information used E (M S V)	SC (M S V)
"Because I'm years older," Hannah smirked.	✓ ✓ ✓ ✓ R ✓ ✓ .		
He gave up arguing and stomped off towards his	✓ ✓ ✓ ✓ ✓ ✓ ✓ ✓		
room. "See you in the morning," he said to	bedroom. She | SC ✓ ✓ ✓ ✓ ✓ ✓ room. See |	Ⓜ Ⓢ Ⓥ / Ⓜ Ⓢ Ⓥ	M S Ⓥ
his mother to emphasize that he was ignoring	✓ ✓ and | SC emphases ✓ R ✓ ✓ ✓ to | emphasize	Ⓜ Ⓢ V / M S Ⓥ	M S Ⓥ
Hannah.	Anna | SC. Hannah. |	Ⓜ Ⓢ Ⓥ	M S Ⓥ
He posed in front of his bedroom mirror. If	✓ possed ✓ ✓ ✓ ✓ ✓ . ✓ posed	M S Ⓥ	
Hannah was a damsel in distress, she couldn't	✓ ✓ ✓ ✓ district | SC ✓ ✓ distress |	M S Ⓥ / Ⓜ Ⓢ Ⓥ	
expect him to come galloping to her rescue.	✓ ✓ ✓ ✓ ✓ ✓ ✓ .		
She could stay tied to the stake. He would	✓ ✓ ✓ died | SC ✓ ✓ . ✓ ✓ tied |	M S Ⓥ / Ⓜ Ⓢ Ⓥ	
charge in cutting this way and that with his	✓ ✓ ✓ the ✓ ✓ ✓ ✓ ✓ this	M Ⓢ Ⓥ	
fearsome sword. All would fall before him and	✓ sWord | SC. ✓ ✓ ✓ ✓ ✓ sword. |	M S Ⓥ / Ⓜ Ⓢ V	
he would fight his way to where she was tied	✓ ✓ ✓ ✓ ✓ ✓ ✓ ✓		
and then …	✓ ✓ …		

Her teacher summarised the analysis of the reading like this:

Claire uses meaning, structure and visual information, reruns occasionally, self-corrects most of her errors, picking up more visual information, and attempts all words.

Claire needs to take more responsibility for making all the information match. She needs to be encouraged to recognise when meaning is lost, and self-correct.

7 Interpreting the Running Record

There is another level of analysis that will help teachers to work out what information in the text the reader is attending to. To do this you must give closer attention to analysing the error and self-correction behaviours. The analysis takes very little time but it can uncover some important things about the reading process.

Readers of text appear to make decisions about the quality of the message they are getting. One kind of theory would say the child is recalling words and attacking words; another kind of theory would say that the child is using information of various kinds to make a choice among possible responses. He is trying to get the best fit with the limited knowledge he has. It is this last kind of theory that guides the following discussion.

Look at the errors in the record

It is important to analyse every error and not to look at errors selectively. Ask yourself, 'What led the child to do (or say) that?' For every error ask yourself at least three questions:

M — Did the meaning or the messages of the text influence the error? Perhaps the reader brought a different meaning to the author's text.

S — Did the structure (syntax) of the sentence up to the error influence the response?

V — Did visual information from the print influence any part of the error?

(See page 24 for explanation of the V category.)

When an error is made write the letters MSV in the error column. Circle the letters if the child's error showed that the child could have used meaning, structure or visual information (which will include letter form and/or letter-sound relationships) from the sentence so far.

Scan the record to answer two other questions

1   Did the child's oral language produce the error, with no influence from the print?

2   Was the child clearly getting some phonemic information from the printed letters?
    What makes you suspect this?

These two questions cannot be used in scoring a record because teachers cannot agree upon their interpretations, and the information is therefore unreliable. However, if the reader sometimes responds as if he was 'just talking', or if specific phonemic information is, without question, used, teachers can note these things in their records but not include them in the formal summation of text reading.

Now look at self-corrections

Often readers make errors and without any prompting, work on the text in some way and self-correct the errors. It is as if they had a feeling that something was not quite right. It is now easy to record in the self-correction column whether the *extra* information the reader added to make the self-correction was meaning, structure or visual information. This is usually rather interesting, especially when we look at what happens across the entire record. A single error could have been unusual for the reader.

Consider the pattern of responses

Now look at the overall pattern of the responses you have circled so that you can bring your analysis of errors and self-corrections together into a written summary. This statement about the sources of information used and neglected will be useful to guide subsequent teaching.

Record the statement at the top of the Running Record next to the appropriate level of the text.

Some common faults

1   Analysis of meaning, structure and visual information is of little value unless it is done carefully.

2   Consider the sentence only up to the error (not the unread text).

3   The total number of M, S or V circles are merely a guide to what is being neglected, what is made a priority, and when the reader can combine different kinds of processing.

Example of a Running Record taken on the Running Record Sheet

RUNNING RECORD SHEET

Name: __Sam__   Date: __4·2·00__   D. of B.: __1·5·94__ Age: __5__ yrs __9__ mths

School: __Westleigh__   Recorder __C.B.__

Text Titles	Errors / Running Words	Error Ratio	Accuracy Rate	Self-correction Ratio
Easy _____	_____	1: _____	_____ %	1. _____
Instructional __Dogs (Highgate/P.M.)(seen)__	$\frac{3}{34}$	1: __11·3__	__90__ %	1: __2__
Hard _____	_____	1: _____	_____ %	1: _____

Directional movement _____✓_____

Analysis of Errors and Self-corrections
Information used or neglected [Meaning (M), Structure or Syntax (S), Visual (V)]

Easy _____

Instructional __Meaning and structure are used predominantly for substitutions with some attention to visual information. Repetition with visual information led to three self-corrections.__

Hard _____

Cross-checking on information (Note that this behaviour changes over time)

Meaning & structure cross-checked with visual information   dogs little / like small

Page	Title: Dogs	E	SC	E MSV	SC MSV
2	$\frac{s-}{Some}$ |T ✓ ✓ ✓	1		M S Ⓥ	
3	✓ ✓ ✓ ✓				
4	✓ ✓ ✓ $\frac{scary}{growly}$	1		Ⓜ Ⓢ V	
5	✓ $\frac{dogs}{like}$ |R|sc ✓ ✓		1	Ⓜ Ⓢ V	M S Ⓥ
6	✓ ✓ ✓ ✓				
7	✓ ✓ ✓ $\frac{little}{Small}$ |R|sc		1	Ⓜ Ⓢ V	M S Ⓥ
8	✓ ✓ $\frac{dog\ is}{dog's}$ |R|sc ✓ ✓		1	Ⓜ Ⓢ Ⓥ	M Ⓢ Ⓥ
	✓ ✓ $\frac{biggest}{cuddliest}$ |R|A|T ✓ ✓	1		Ⓜ Ⓢ V	
		3	3	5 5 2	1 3

Read slowly with some intonation.

8 Understanding the Reading Process

When teachers ask themselves, 'What does my record tell me?', they bring their own beliefs about literacy (their personal theory of literacy/learning) and their background of professional experience into the interpretation. Interpretations of Running Records are heavily weighted with the theoretical view the teacher already holds. My interpretations fit with my theory that progress depends on an increasing complexity in the processing which enables the reader to read more difficult texts. I think of the child working with several different types of knowledge lying there in the print (which I call 'different kinds of information').

To explain the error consider the behaviour up to the point of the error.

To explain a self-correction consider what might have led the child to spontaneously correct the error.

If teachers bring different theories to these records they may ask quite different questions of the data and their interpretations may seem different. However, the behaviour record would still look the same because it comes from extensive research into what young readers do as they read text.

For example, examine the attention given in these analyses to V, standing for the visual information in print. During acquisition the visual information becomes intricately linked to phonemic information (the sounds of speech or phonology) so that children could probably be said to 'hear' a letter or cluster of letters they are looking at. Theorists tell us that visual information also links directly to a vocabulary of known words (spelling patterns or orthography). So, theoretically, the symbol V in the analysis of Running Records stands for the stimulus information on the page of print irrespective of whether the processing is through a phonological system or a visual system. This is a point at which teachers might differ in their 'understanding' of what a reader was doing.

What if a reliable behaviour record does not support expectations? Unable to deny that the actual behaviour did occur we probably need to adjust any assumptions that are not supported by recorded data. So it is important that we have reliable records.

Running Records are useful if we remember the following things.

- Record error behaviour in full because the information is needed when interpreting the records.
- Poor observation will reduce the number of errors and inflate the accuracy score.
- Reliability drops as accuracy levels fall because there is more error to be recorded.
- Observation of poor readers is difficult and requires rigorous training to reach agreement on scoring because of the complexity of the error behaviour.
- The most reliable records would be obtained by scoring an observation immediately following its manual recording but for classroom teachers that is not usually possible.

In older readers look for different signs of progress

If Running Records are used with older readers there should be a special reason for taking them. They are excellent for recording the early phases of literacy acquisition but before long what the reader is doing becomes too fast and too sophisticated for teachers to observe in real time. Literacy processing shifts gradually towards this.

As the reader learns to process more information more quickly, behaviours change and new things can be noted. Errors occur even though the reader clearly used meaning, structure and visual information to get to a response (*strong* for *sturdy*). It is an important 'sign of progress' when errors do contain several kinds of correct information even though the final decision is not quite correct.

Another change occurs when more proficient readers utter only the word beginning and then give the whole word. These are examples:

    wu/would   pl/play   Pe/Peter   bu/but

A similar kind of thing happens when the older reader corrects what might have been an error before giving the whole word, as in:

    m.../parents   gar.../ground   d.../tied

Sometimes there is more repetition as the older reader tries to regroup words in phrases.

In older readers self-correction occurs less frequently. In theory we suppose that it has 'gone underground' and the reader is correcting errors before saying them. If the teacher introduces a more challenging text the process of self-correcting may reappear. Even adults reading aloud can be heard to self-correct.

Records of Individual and Group Progress

Education is primarily concerned with change in the learning of individuals, yet educators rarely document change over time in individuals as they learn. It is not difficult to collect evidence of change over time in early literacy learning, particularly from young children at the beginning of formal education.

Rochelle's progress at two observation points

Book Level	Progress
1	
2	
3	
4	
5	Time 1 (date)
6	*The Escalator* (easy)
7	*Going to School* (instructional)
8	*Playtime* (hard)
9	
10	
11	
12	Time 2 (date)
13	*The Pet Show* (easy)
14	*A Wet Morning* (instructional)
15	*Hungry Lambs* (hard)
16	
17	
18	
19	

Two ways of using Running Records to capture individual progress over time are shown. In Rochelle's case the teacher grouped the books that her class read into approximate levels of difficulty and placed numbers for these levels at the left side of her sheet. Then she took her Running Records of Rochelle's reading on two occasions several months apart, and she entered the names of the books Rochelle found easy, instructional or hard. Rochelle's progress is clear.

A different record was kept by the teacher who was keeping a close watch on Joan's progress by monitoring it frequently. This teacher used the Record of Book Level sheet (page 32) and entered the date of the observation along the horizontal line. She chose to take a record once a week. She entered an open circle for the instructional level of text read because no story at a higher level of text reached the 90 percent accuracy criterion. The next week she raised the text difficulty level and Joan's accuracy fell below 90 percent and so she used a black circle on her graph. In two more weeks of teaching she raised the difficulty level again. (Meanwhile Joan read several new texts but all at the same level of difficulty.) From then onwards as the teacher raised the text difficulty Joan was able to take the challenge except for once after a holiday break.

A teacher may follow several different children on the same graph, using the same plotting procedures. There are problems of clustering if the children are homogeneous in their progress. Such a graph will show many things about individual differences: in starting levels, in paths of progress, in fast or slow 'take-off' in the programme and in final outcome levels.

She would quickly identify children who were working on material that was too difficult, preventing them from working in the context of mostly correct reading, or children who temporarily needed more of her attention.

A weekly record of Joan's progress

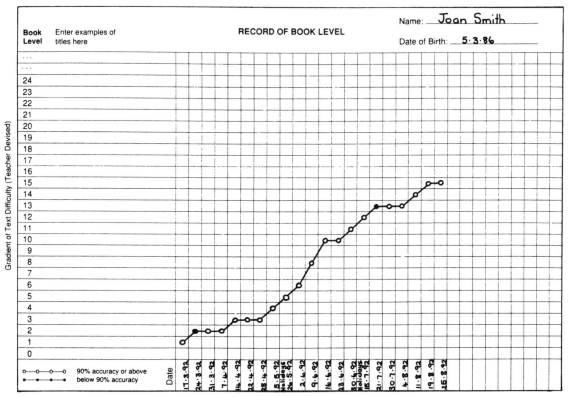

Teachers may follow the progress of several children

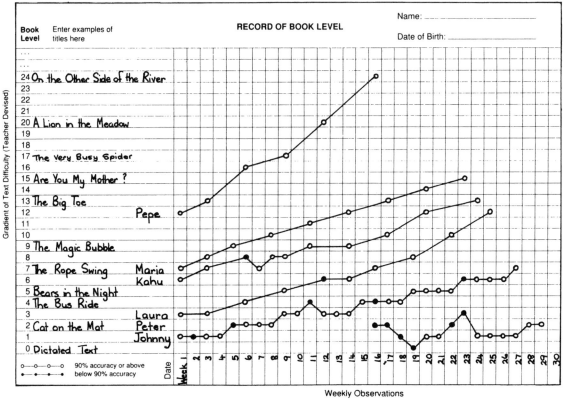

The Record of Book Level sheet is on page 32.

10 Making Decisions About Instruction

Teachers will find many uses for Running Records.

School entry checks

Teachers will have their own ways of collecting and recording information about learners from the time they enter school. Running Records can even be taken on the child's earliest attempts to read little books, enriching the teacher's observations. Sometimes education systems select particular literacy processes for a baseline assessment, but a range of tasks is much more likely to capture the areas that reveal the strengths of individual children. *An Observation Survey of Early Literacy Achievement*, from which Running Records have been extracted, is such a broad-ranging survey.

For teaching individuals

Using the Running Record for teaching purposes teachers might:
- first try to find a book level appropriate for a child,
- check a child after a series of lessons,
- evaluate whether a lift in text level is appropriate,
- observe particular difficulties in particular children,
- place a child shifting group, class or school,
- add to a record monitoring progress over time.

For teaching groups

Using the Running Record for informing group instruction:
- teachers might group children who could work together at this time,
- teachers could evaluate progress and see when regrouping is desirable,
- teachers would see how different the processing of particular children was and adjust attention within the group to suit individual learners.

Running Records can be used with older readers providing oral reading is what we want to observe (Johnston, 1997).

11 Evidence of Emphasis: What Things Get Attention in Your Programme?

If teachers take records of text reading with a wide sample of children they will quickly discover emphases and neglects in the class instruction. Word-by-word reading, sounding out words in single phonemes, not attending to meaning and reading nonsense, ignoring first-letter cues or not going beyond these, or not attending to detail in the middle of a word — if any of these persist longer than they should they may show up as a problem for a group of learners. On the other hand good outcomes may show up with getting it all together smoothly, or working on new words in ways that surprise and impress the teacher, enjoying the stories and commenting on the characters and the plot, for example.

If the programme is changed so that new emphases are introduced, like a shift to asking for more fluent, natural reading, then Running Records can be used to monitor whether the change is having the desired effect.

Recommended Reading

Clay, M.M. (1993). *An Observation Survey of Early Literacy Achievement*. Auckland: Heinemann.

Clay, M.M. (2000). *Concepts About Print*. Auckland: Heinemann.

Fountas, Irene and Pinnell, Gay Su (1996). *Guided Reading*. Portsmouth, NH: Heinemann.

Johnston, P.J. (1997). *Knowing Literacy*. York, Maine: Stenhouse Press.

Johnston, P.J. (2000). *Running Records: A Self-tutoring Guide*. York, Maine: Stenhouse Press.

RUNNING RECORD SHEET

Name: _____ Date: _____ D. of B.: _____ Age: _____ yrs _____ mths

School: _____ Recorder _____

Text Titles	$\dfrac{\text{Errors}}{\text{Running Words}}$	Error Ratio	Accuracy Rate	Self-correction Ratio
Easy _____	_____	1: _____	_____ %	1: _____
Instructional _____	_____	1: _____	_____ %	1: _____
Hard _____	_____	1: _____	_____ %	1: _____

Directional movement _____

Analysis of Errors and Self-corrections
Information used or neglected [Meaning (M), Structure or Syntax (S), Visual (V)]

Easy _____

Instructional _____

_____

_____

Hard _____

_____

Cross-checking on information (Note that this behaviour changes over time)

Page	Title	Count		Analysis of Errors and Self-corrections — Information used	
		E	SC	E MSV	SC MSV

Page		Count		Analysis of Errors and Self-corrections
		E	SC	**Information used**
				E MSV	SC MSV
		E	SC	E MSV	SC MSV

RECORD OF BOOK LEVEL

Name: _____

Date of Birth: _____

Book Level	Enter examples of titles here
⋮	
⋮	
24	
23	
22	
21	
20	
19	
18	
17	
16	
15	
14	
13	
12	
11	
10	
9	
8	
7	
6	
5	
4	
3	
2	
1	
0	
Date	

Gradient of Text Difficulty (Teacher Devised)

o—o—o o   90% accuracy or above

•—•—• •   below 90% accuracy

Weekly Observations